OLD LONDON ENGRAVINGS

OLD HYDE PARK CORNER IN 1820. *From Mr. Crace's Collection.*

Lang**Syne**
PUBLISHING
WRITING *to* REMEMBER

79 Main Street, Newtongrange,
Midlothian EH22 4NA
Tel: 0131 344 0414   Fax: 0845 075 6085
E-mail: info@lang-syne.co.uk
www.langsyneshop.co.uk

Design by Dorothy Meikle
Printed by 1010 Printing International Ltd
© Lang Syne Publishers Ltd 2016

ISBN 978-1-85217-653-2

INTRODUCTION

In the following pages we journey through the London of our forefathers via dozens of beautiful engravings which span centuries.

We see what many world-famous places in the heart of the capital were like and we also travel out to the suburbs for revealing glimpses of life in times past.

The front cover features a view of St. Paul's Cathedral and St. Martin's-Le-Grand, 1760, and the rear cover shows Old View of St. James's Palace before the Great Fire of London; March of the Archers; and The Coronation Procession of Anne Boleyn to Westminster Abbey.

These engravings were originally published in "Old and New London" (1873-8) by Messrs. Cassell, Petter, Galpin and Co., London, Paris and New York. This was a six volume work written in part by Walter Thornbury who traced the city's origins from the earliest times.

Engravings for this special edition coloured from the original monochrome in 2015 by Ian Cramer.

HYDE PARK CORNER IN 1750. *From Mr. Crace's Collection.*

HYDE PARK ON SUNDAY. *From a Print published in 1804.*

A MEET OF THE FOUR-IN-HAND CLUB.

BUCKINGHAM PALACE : GARDEN FRONT.

BUCKINGHAM HOUSE IN 1775.

ST. JAMES'S SQUARE IN 1773.

VIEW OF ST. JAMES'S PALACE, TIME OF QUEEN ANNE. *From an Old Engraving.*

WESTMINSTER FROM THE ROOF OF WHITEHALL. *From a View published by Smith, 1807.*

WESTMINSTER HALL. *From a View published by J.T. Smith, 1808.*

OLD WHITEHALL PALACE FROM THE RIVER.

WESTMINSTER FROM THE GARDENS OF SOMERSET HOUSE, 1750. *After a View by Canaletto.*

LEICESTER SQUARE, ABOUT 1750.

SCOTLAND YARD, ABOUT 1720.

COVENT GARDEN MARKET, ABOUT 1820.

COVENT GARDEN IN 1660.

ANCIENT VIEW OF CHEAPSIDE.
From La Serre's "Entrée de la Reyne Mére du Roy", showing the Procession of Mary de Medicis.

BOW CHURCH AND CHEAPSIDE IN 1750. *From a Print in Mr. Crace's Collection.*

ST. PAUL'S AND THE NEIGHBOURHOOD IN 1540. *From a Copy, in the possession of J.G. Crace, Esq., of the earliest known view of London, taken by Van der Wyngarde for Philip II of Spain.*

PART OF INNER TEMPLE, 1800. *From a Drawing in Mr. Crace's Collection.*

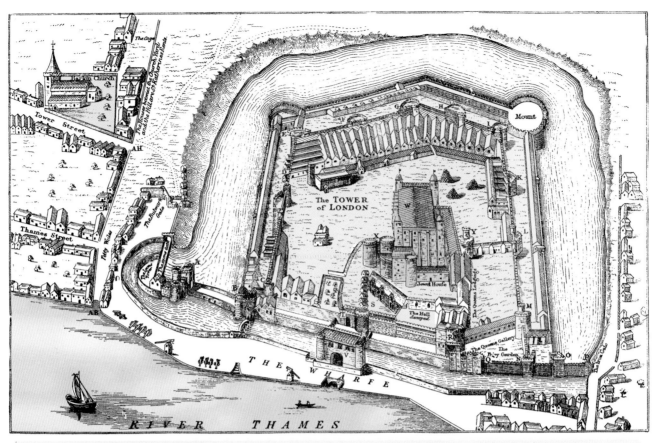

THE TOWER. *From a Survey made in 1597 by W. Haiward and J. Gascoyne.*

A. Middle Tower.   B. Tower at the Gate.   C. Bell Tower.   D. Beauchamp Tower.   E. Devilin Tower.   F. Flint Tower.   G. Bowyer Tower.   H. Brick Tower.   J. Martin Tower.   K. Constable Tower.
L. Broad Arrow Tower.   M. Salt Tower.   N. Well Tower.   O. Tower leading to Iron Gate.   P. Tower above Iron Gate.   Q. Cradle Tower.   R. Lantern Tower.   S. Hall Tower.   T. Bloody Tower.
V. St. Thomas's Tower.   W. Caesar's, or White Tower.   X. Cole Harbour.   Y. Wardrobe Tower.   A.B. House at Water Gate, called the Ram's Head.   A.H. End of Tower Street.

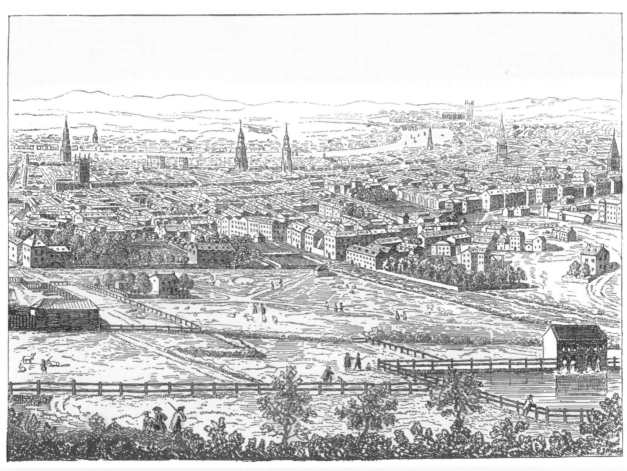

LONDON FROM CLERKENWELL (WEST END). *From a View by Canaletto published in 1753.*

ISLINGTON IN 1780.

PETTICOAT LANE.

THE TOWER OF LONDON. *From a View published about 1700.*

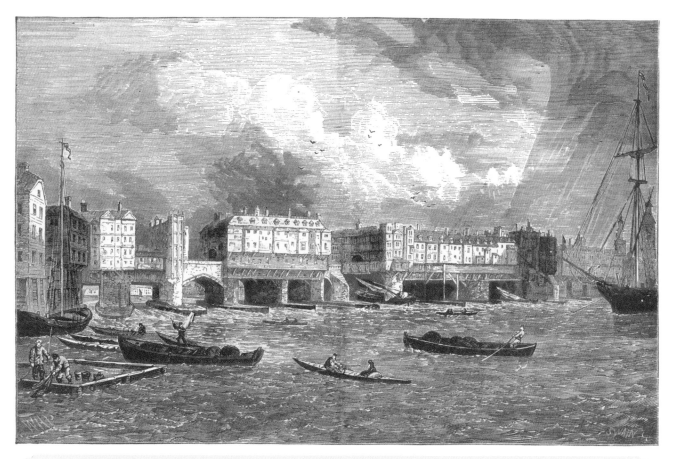

LONDON BRIDGE, 1756. *From an Old View, taken shortly before the Demolition of the Houses.*

SOUTHWARK FAIR. *After Hogarth's Picture.*

HAMMERSMITH MALL IN 1800.

GOLDEN SQUARE IN 1750.

OXFORD MARKET IN 1870.

QUEEN SQUARE IN 1810.

GROSVENOR SQUARE.

FARM IN THE REGENT'S PARK, 1750.

TURNPIKE IN THE HAMPSTEAD ROAD, AND ST. JAMES'S CHURCH IN 1820.

HIGHGATE FROM UPPER HOLLOWAY. *From Chatelain, 1745.*

HIGHGATE ARCHWAY GATE AND TAVERN IN 1825. *From an Original Sketch.*

VIEW FROM "MOLL KING'S HOUSE", HAMPSTEAD IN 1760.

POND STREET, HAMPSTEAD IN 1750.

CHURCH ROW, HAMPSTEAD IN 1750.

HAMPSTEAD HEATH IN 1840. *From a Drawing by Constable.*

GENERAL VIEW OF OLD KENTISH TOWN IN 1820.

The **IDLE PRENTICE** Executed at Tyburn.

THE IDLE APPRENTICE EXECUTED AT TYBURN. *After Hogarth's Print.*

23

THE CONSUMPTION HOSPITAL, BROMPTON.

NOTTING HILL IN 1750.

THE ROTUNDA, RANELAGH GARDENS IN 1750.

"JENNY'S WHIM" BRIDGE IN 1750.

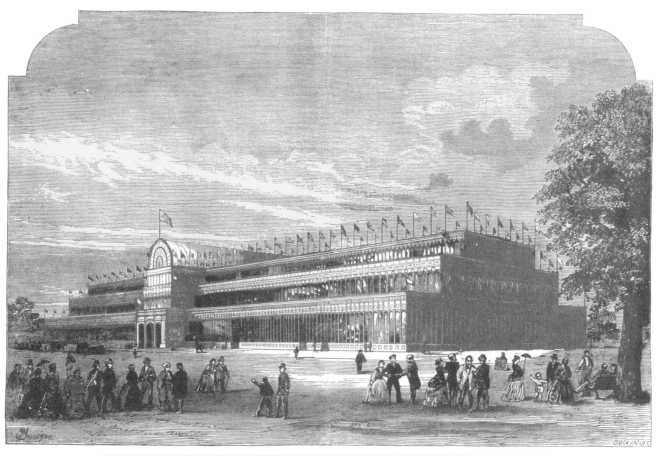

EXTERIOR OF THE GREAT EXHIBITION OF 1851.

THE NORTH SIDE OF KNIGHTSBRIDGE IN 1820, FROM THE CANNON
BREWERY TO HYDE PARK CORNER. *From a Drawing in Mr. Crace's Collection.*

THE MARYLEBONE SCHOOL HOUSE IN 1780.

BLOOMSBURY SQUARE.

UNIVERSITY COLLEGE, GOWER STREET.

TYBURN TURNPIKE IN 1820.

BERKELEY SQUARE.

HANOVER SQUARE IN 1750.

FRONT OF THE BRITISH MUSEUM IN 1880.

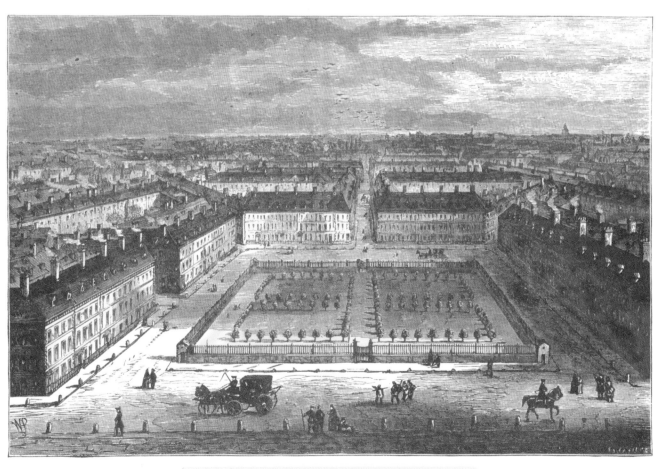

RED LION SQUARE IN 1780.

INTERIOR OF THE MINT. *From a Drawing about 1820.*

ST. KATHARINE'S DOCKS.

LONDON FROM CLERKENWELL (CITY AND EAST END).
From a View by Canaletto published in 1753.

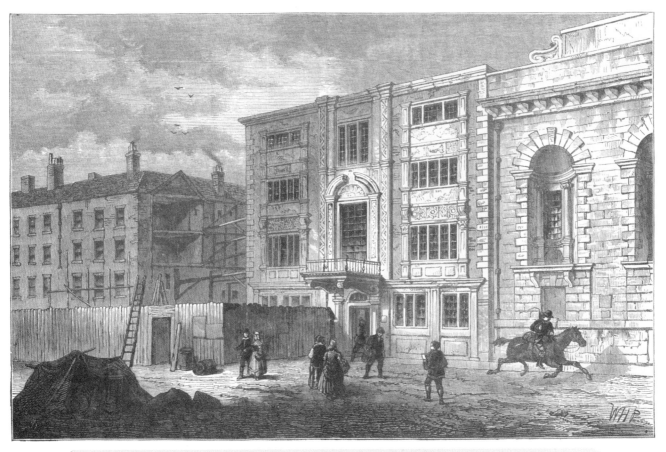

THE OLD POST OFFICE IN LOMBARD STREET, ABOUT 1800.

CORNHILL IN 1630. *From a View published by Boydell.*

THE OLD CUSTOM HOUSE. *From a View by Maurer published in 1753.*

HOLBORN VALLEY AND SNOW HILL PREVIOUS TO THE CONSTRUCTION OF THE VIADUCT.

INTERIOR OF THE FLEET PRISON – THE RACKET COURT.

CHARTERHOUSE SQUARE. *From an Old Print.*

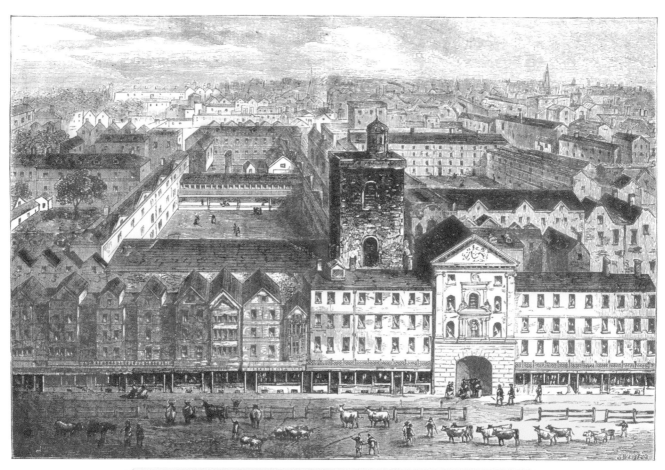

ST. BARTHOLOMEW'S HOSPITAL IN 1750.

LAMBETH PALACE FROM THE RIVER IN 1709.

KENNINGTON COMMON AND CHURCH IN 1830.

MIDDLE ROW, HOLBORN. *From a Drawing taken shortly before its Demolition, 1865.*

CLERKENWELL GREEN IN 1789.

SOUTH EAST VIEW OF LONDON IN 1550. *From an Engraving by Wood in Mr. Crace's Collection.*

HOARE'S OLD BANKING HOUSE. *From a Drawing by Shepherd, 1838 in Mr. Crace's Collection.*

THE STOCKS' MARKET, SITE OF THE MANSION HOUSE. *From an Old Print.*

THE SECOND ROYAL EXCHANGE, CORNHILL.

DIVIDEND DAY AT THE BANK IN 1770.

THE ROYAL BANQUET IN GUILDHALL. *From a Contemporary Print.*

OLD WESTMINSTER BRIDGE IN 1754.

CHARING CROSS FROM NORTHUMBERLAND HOUSE IN 1750.

YORK STAIRS AND THE WATER TOWER. *From a Print dated 1780.*

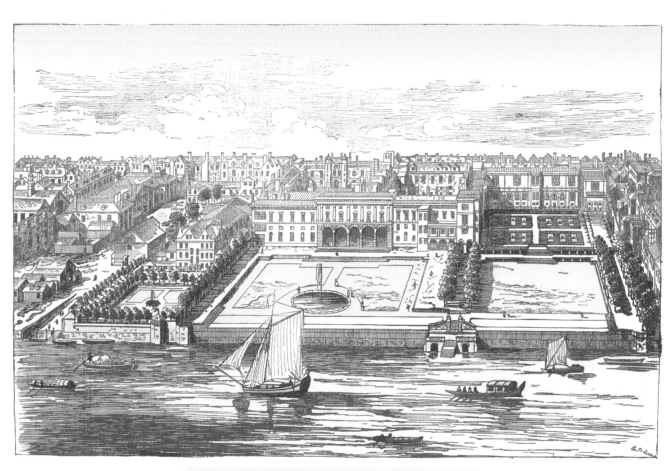

SOMERSET HOUSE IN 1755.

OLD COCKSPUR STREET.

NORTHUMBERLAND HOUSE. *From a View by Canaletto.*

INTERIOR OF THE HOUSE OF COMMONS IN 1834.

INTERIOR OF OLD WESTMINSTER HALL. *From a Print published in 1797.*

THE ROYAL DOCKYARD, DEPTFORD IN 1810.

DEPTFORD AND GREENWICH IN 1815.

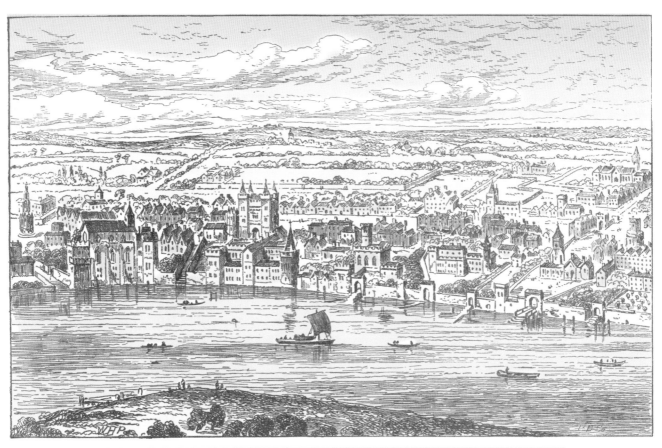

LONDON FROM TEMPLE BAR TO CHARING CROSS.
From Van der Wyngarde's View A.D. 1543.

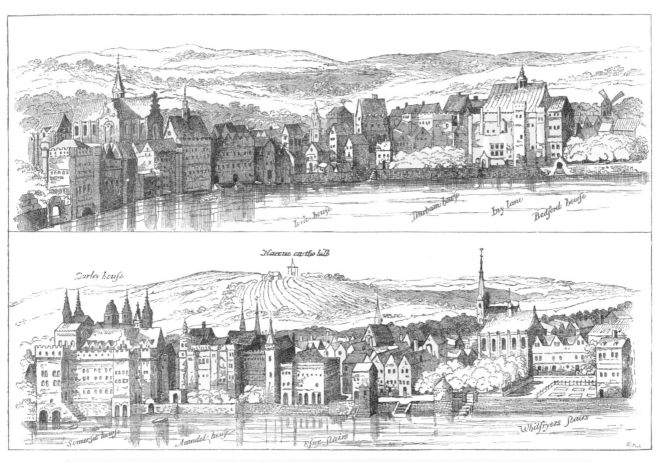

THE STRAND FROM THE THAMES, SIXTEENTH CENTURY.

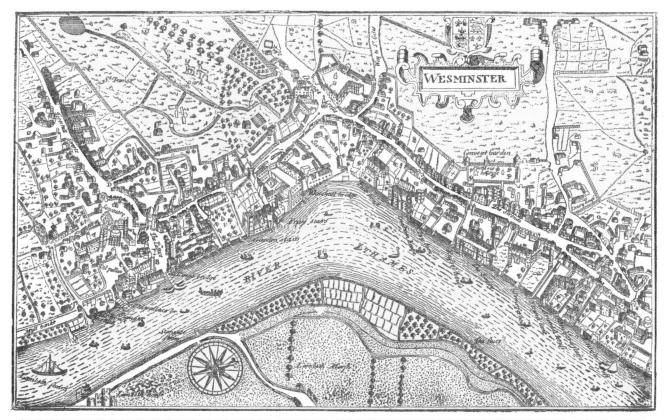

PLAN OF WESTMINSTER. *From Norden's Survey, taken in Queen Elizabeth's Reign, 1593.*
A. The Abbey.   B. Westminster Hall.   D. Long Ditch.   E. Thieving Lane.   F. The Amnerie.   G. Way to Tothill Fields.
H. The Lord Dacres.   K. King Street.   L. Round Woolstaple.   M. The Park Lodgings.   N. The Tilt Yard.
O. St. Martin's-in-the-Fields.   P. Clement's Lane.   Q. New Inn.   R. St. Clement Danes.   S. Temple Bar.

EXECUTION OF THE CONSPIRATORS IN THE GUNPOWDER PLOT IN THE YEAR 1606.
From a Print published in 1795.

MARGARET STREET, WESTMINSTER. *From a sketch made in 1820.*

WHITEHALL, LOOKING TOWARDS THE HOLBEIN GATEWAY. *From a View by Maurer, 1753.*

THE EMBANKMENT FROM CHARING CROSS BRIDGE.

SOHO SQUARE, ABOUT 1700.

ST. JAMES'S STREET IN 1750. *From an Original Drawing in Mr. Crace's Collection.*

OLD HOUSES IN PALL MALL, ABOUT 1830. *From an Original Drawing in Mr. Crace's Collection.*

FROST FAIR ON THE THAMES IN 1683.

FROST ON THE THAMES IN 1814.

OLD HUNGERFORD MARKET. *From a View published in 1805.*

HUNGERFORD MARKET FROM THE BRIDGE IN 1850.

THE SAVOY IN 1650. *From a very scarce Etching by Hollar.*

ON THE THAMES AT LOW WATER.

HALL OF THE ROYAL COLLEGE OF SURGEONS.

THE "COCK AND MAGPIE", DRURY LANE. *From an Original Sketch, 1840.*

A LORD MAYOR AND HIS LADY (MIDDLE OF THE 17TH CENTURY). *From an Old Print.*

THE DEMOLITION OF CHEAPSIDE CROSS. *From an Old Print.*

ROASTING THE RUMPS IN FLEET STREET. *From an Old Print.*

FLEET STREET, THE TEMPLE, ETC. *From a Plan published by Ralph Aggas, 1563.*

ENTRANCE TO THE HOUSE OF LORDS IN 1780.

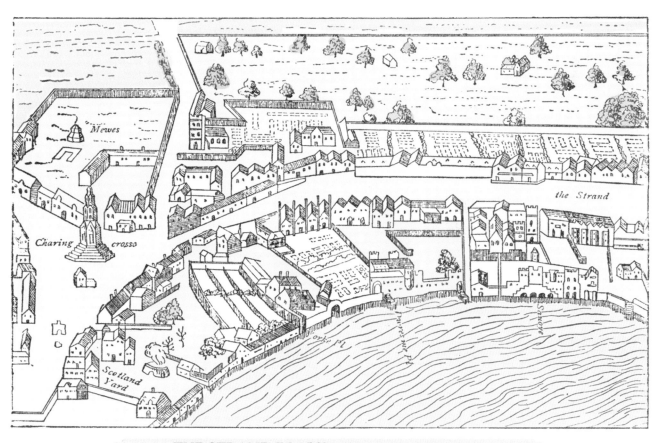

THE STRAND IN 1560. *From the Map of Ralph Aggas.*

INTERIOR OF COVENT GARDEN THEATRE IN 1804.

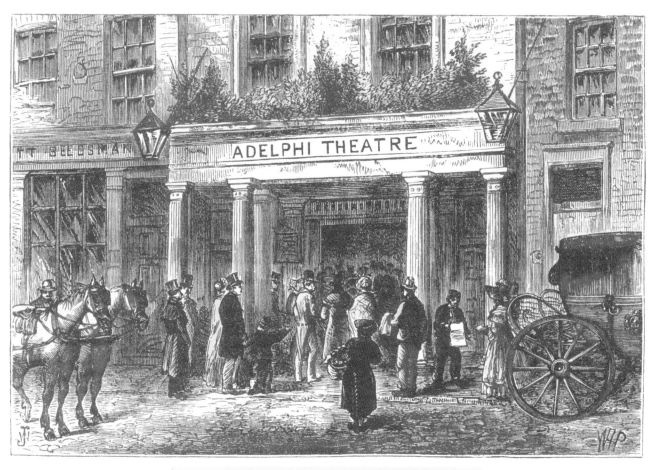

THE OLD ADELPHI THEATRE.

OLD SMITHFIELD MARKET IN 1837.

PLACE OF EXECUTION IN OLD SMITHFIELD.

RAY STREET, CLERKENWELL, ABOUT 1860.

GUY FAWKES AND THE CONSPIRATORS. *From a Contemporary Print.*

BILLINGSGATE. *From a View taken in 1820.*

THE ORIGINAL PRIORY CHURCH OF ST. JOHN, CLERKENWELL.

DYERS' HALL IN 1850.

THE CHURCH OF ALLHALLOWS THE GREAT IN 1784.

LONDON DANDY OF 1646.

FRONT OF MONTAGU HOUSE, GREAT RUSSELL STREET IN 1830.

FRONT OF OLD DRURY LANE THEATRE.

CAVENDISH SQUARE IN 1820.

THE ENTRANCE TO PORTLAND PLACE IN 1815.

STRATFORD PLACE.

THE "FARTHING PIE HOUSE". *From a Drawing, 1820.*

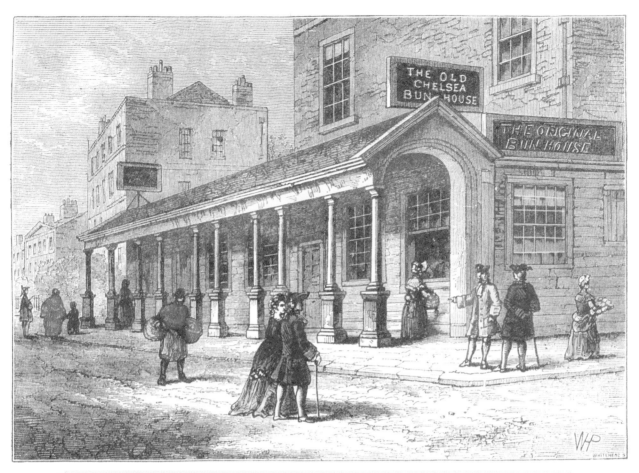

THE CHELSEA BUN-HOUSE IN 1810. *From Mr. Crace's Collection.*

CHELSEA WATER-WORKS IN 1750.

SALE OF HYDE PARK TURNPIKE.

THE "WHITE HART", KNIGHTSBRIDGE IN 1820.

THE PLACE OF EXECUTION, TYBURN IN 1750.

EXECUTION OF LORD FERRERS AT TYBURN. *From an Old Print of the Period.*

OLD KENSINGTON CHURCH, ABOUT 1750.

OLD VIEW OF KENSINGTON, ABOUT 1750.

THE "CASTLE" TAVERN, KENTISH TOWN ROAD IN 1800.

THE ASSEMBLY ROOMS, KENTISH TOWN IN 1750.

THE PADDINGTON CANAL IN 1840.

THE "PLOUGH" AT KENSAL GREEN IN 1820.

CAMDEN TOWN FROM THE HAMPSTEAD ROAD, MARYLEBONE IN 1780.

LORD'S GROUND IN 1837.

HACKNEY, LOOKING TOWARDS THE CHURCH IN 1840.

FORTIFICATIONS OF OLD ST. PANCRAS.

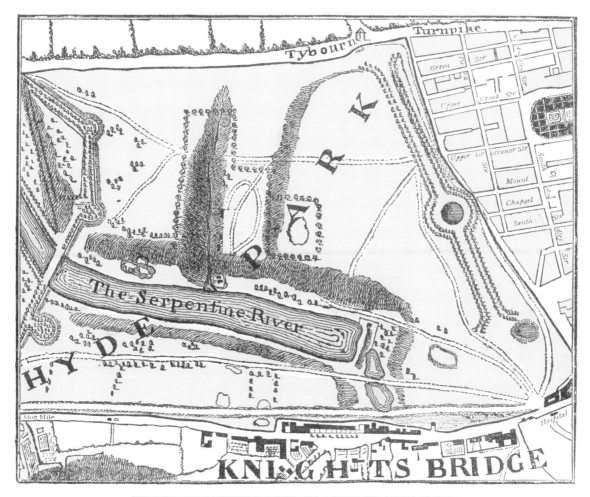

HYDE PARK. *From Rocque's Map, 1748.*

ENTRANCE TO GROSVENOR STREET FROM HYDE PARK, ABOUT 1780.

THE MARBLE ARCH.

THE FRONT OF GROSVENOR HOUSE.

CHEAPSIDE CROSS AS IT APPEARED IN 1547.
Showing part of the Procession of Edward VI to his Coronation, from a Painting of the Time.

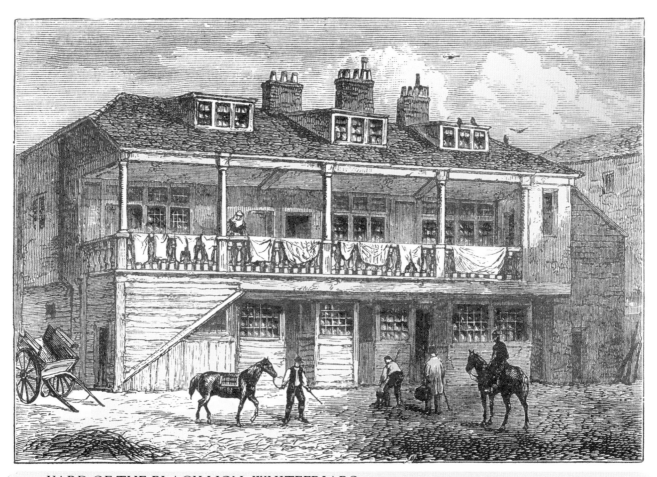

YARD OF THE BLACK LION, WHITEFRIARS. *From a Drawing, 1859 in Mr. Crace's Collection.*

THE LORD MAYOR'S PROCESSION. *From Hogarth's "Industrious Apprentice".*

EXTERIOR OF GOLDSMITHS' HALL.

THE CHAPEL ROYAL, WHITEHALL, EXTERIOR.

EXETER CHANGE IN 1826.

THE KING STREET GATEWAY, WHITEHALL.

COACHES : REIGN OF QUEEN ANNE.

COVENT GARDEN MARKET LOOKING EASTWARD. *From a Print of 1786.*

BURNING OF COVENT GARDEN THEATRE IN 1856.

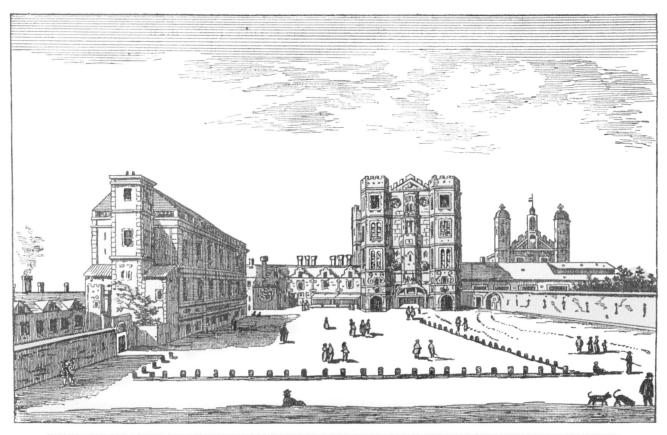

WHITEHALL, ABOUT 1650. *From a Copy by Smith of a Rare Print by Israel Silvestre.*

WHITEHALL YARD.

FLEET MARKET, ABOUT 1800. *From a Drawing in Mr. Gardner's Collection.*

KING'S CROSS. *From a View taken during its Demolition in 1845.*

TEMPLE BAR AND THE "DEVIL TAVERN".

THE TEMPLE STAIRS IN 1680.

OLD OUTFALL OF THE SERPENTINE AT KNIGHTSBRIDGE IN 1800.
From Mr. Crace's Collection.

BRIDGE OVER THE SERPENTINE.

THE CAKE-HOUSE, HYDE PARK. *From a Drawing in Mr. Crace's Collection.*

GROUP OF OLD TREES IN HYDE PARK.

CAMBRIDGE HOUSE IN 1854.

DEVONSHIRE HOUSE, ABOUT 1800.

THE ROYAL INSTITUTION.

HAMILTON PLACE IN 1802. *From a Drawing in the Guildhall Library.*

BURLINGTON HOUSE IN 1875.

ENCAMPMENT IN THE GARDENS OF MONTAGU HOUSE, 1780.

LONG'S HOTEL, BOND STREET.

GLOUCESTER HOUSE, PICCADILLY.

THE "ADAM AND EVE" TAVERN IN 1750.

THE MANOR HOUSE OF TOTEN HALL.
From a View published by Wilkinson, 1813.

EXTERIOR OF THE TOTTENHAM STREET THEATRE IN 1830.

THE MIDDLESEX HOSPITAL.

THE YARD OF THE OLD "WHITE BEAR" INN, PICCADILLY, ABOUT 1820.
From an Original Drawing by Shepherd in Mr. Crace's Collection.

TURKISH BATH, JERMYN STREET.

TOTTENHAM MILLS

RECTORY HOUSE

GEORGE & VULTURE

W H PRIOR

VIEWS IN TOTTENHAM.

THE "HALFWAY HOUSE", KENSINGTON IN 1850.

THE OLD TURNPIKE, KENSINGTON IN 1820.

WEST FRONT OF KENSINGTON PALACE.

THE ROUND POND, KENSINGTON GARDENS.

KING'S CROSS UNDERGROUND STATION IN 1868.

TRIAL-TRIP ON THE UNDERGROUND RAILWAY, 1863.

THE GATE-HOUSE, HIGHGATE IN 1820. *From an Original Sketch.*

JACK STRAW'S CASTLE.

VIEW IN THE SURREY GARDENS, 1850.

DIVING BELL USED IN THE CONSTRUCTION OF THE THAMES TUNNEL.

KENNINGTON FROM THE GREEN IN 1780.

THE "RED COW" INN, HAMMERSMITH.

THE INDIA OFFICE FROM ST. JAMES'S PARK.

| LORD WORCESTER. | LADY JERSEY. | CLANRONALD MACDONALD. | LADY WORCESTER. |

THE FIRST QUADRILLE DANCED AT "ALMACK'S".
From Gronow's "Reminiscences".

HOUSE IN WESTMINSTER SAID TO HAVE BEEN OCCUPIED BY OLIVER CROMWELL.

THE LONDON UNIVERSITY, BURLINGTON GARDENS.

ENTRANCE TO EUSTON SQUARE STATION.

KINGSTON HOUSE, KNIGHTSBRIDGE.

CHEYNE WALK AND CADOGAN PIER IN 1860.

COURTYARD OF THE "ROSE AND CROWN" IN 1820.

THE OLD MANOR HOUSE, MARY-LE-BONE,
IN THE TIME OF QUEEN ELIZABETH. *From an Old Print.*

WESTMINSTER ABBEY FROM ST. JAMES'S PARK, ABOUT 1740.

THE LORD MAYOR'S BANQUETING-HOUSE,
OXFORD ROAD IN 1750. *From Mr. Crace's Collection.*

HOSPITAL FOR SICK CHILDREN, GREAT ORMOND STREET.

PLAYING AT PALL MALL.

THE MALL IN 1450.

OLD HOUSES IN HOLBORN.

THE OLD "BLACK BULL" INN, GRAY'S INN LANE.

THE SHAKESPEARE GALLERY, PALL MALL. *From a Drawing in Mr. Crace's Collection.*

MARLBOROUGH HOUSE IN 1710. *From a Contemporary Engraving.*

MILK FAIR, ST. JAMES'S PARK.

SCHOMBERG HOUSE IN 1820. *From an Original Drawing in Mr. Crace's Collection.*

AMBASSADORS' COURT, ST. JAMES'S PALACE IN 1875.

KITCHEN OF ST. JAMES'S PALACE IN THE TIME OF GEORGE III.

CORONATION OF GEORGE IV IN WESTMINSTER HALL : THE CHAMPION'S CHALLENGE.

From a Contemporary Engraving in the "Gentleman's Magazine".